GRACE NICHOLS

The Fat Black Woman's Poems

www. hitchcock.itc
(itc)

For John

A *Virago* Book

First published by Virago Press 1984
Reprinted 1985, 1987, 1990, 1991, 1992, 1993, 1994, 2000, 2001

Copyright © Grace Nichols 1984

The sequence from *i is a long memoried woman* is reprinted with kind
permission from Karnak House, 300 Westbourne Park Road,
London W11 1EH

A CIP catalogue record for this book
is available from the British Library

ISBN 0 86068 635 3

Printed and bound in Great Britain by
Clays Ltd, St Ives plc

Virago Press
A Division of
Little, Brown and Company (UK)
Brettenham House
Lancaster Place
London WC2E 7EN

Contents

The Fat Black Woman's Poems

Beauty	7
The Assertion	8
The Fat Black Woman Remembers	9
Alone	10
The Fat Black Woman Goes Shopping	11
Invitation	12
Trap Evasions	14
Thoughts drifting through the fat black woman's head while having a full bubble bath	15
The Fat Black Woman Composes a Black Poem . . .	16
. . . And a Fat Poem	17
The Fat Black Woman's Motto on Her Bedroom Door	18
Tropical Death	19
Looking at Miss World	20
The Fat Black Woman's Instructions to a Suitor	21
The Fat Black Woman Versus Politics	22
Small Questions Asked by the Fat Black Woman	23
Afterword	24

In Spite of Ourselves

Like a Beacon	27
Fear	28
Island Man	29
We New World Blacks	30
Shopping	31
Winter Thoughts	32
Skanking Englishman Between Trains	33
Spring	34
Two Old Black Men on a Leicester Square Park Bench	35
Waiting for Thelma's Laughter	36

Back Home Contemplation

Those Women	39
Childhood	40
Back Home Contemplation	41
Price We Pay for the Sun	42
So the Eagle	43
Praise Song for My Mother	44
Why Shouldn't She?	44
Hey There Now!	45
Candlefly	46
Mango	47
Star-apple	47
Guenips	47
Sea Timeless Song	48
Be a Butterfly	49
Iguana Memory	50

i is a long memoried woman

Waterpot	53
Loveact	54
Skin-teeth	55
Sugar Cane	56
Like a Flame	60
This Kingdom	61
Holding My Beads	63
Epilogue	64

The Fat Black Woman's Poems

Grace Nichols poems evoke three social stereotypes: being fat, being black and being a woman. However such definitions remain controversial so far as her poems constitute an overt attempt to challenge conventional (white) male definitions of black women as well as redefine black females identities in new and unexpected ways.

Nichols ability to create alternative spaces wherein black female experience is to have a transformative impact relies significantly on the commitment to the body as an empowering instrument to express one's subjectivity and desires. Rather than be signified by fixed and stable cultural inscription its 'new' body appears as an active medium that is endlessly constructing itself through multiple acts and heterogeneous meanings. In such a display, the female body becomes a site of semiotic struggle between forces of patriarchal control and feminine resistance, of capitalism and subordination — of desired objects and desiring subjects.

Beauty

Beauty
is a fat black woman
walking the fields
pressing a breezed
hibiscus
to her cheek
while the sun lights up
her feet   *[handwritten: contrast of lighter soles]*

Beauty
is a fat black woman
riding the waves
" drifting in happy oblivion "   *[handwritten: this fat woman wants to do so.]*
while the sea turns back
to hug her shape

The Assertion

woman's body beams

Heavy as a whale
eyes beady with contempt
and a kind of fire of love
the fat black woman sits
on the golden stool
and refuses to move

the white robed chiefs
are resigned
in their postures of resignation

the fat black woman's fingers
are creased in gold
body ringed in folds
pulse beat at her throat

This is my birthright
says the fat black woman
giving a fat black chuckle
showing her fat black toes

interior & exterior are made by the same gesture of defiance and subversion.

The Fat Black Woman Remembers

The fat black woman
remembers her Mama
and them days of playing
the Jovial Jemima

tossing pancakes
to heaven
in smokes of happy hearty
                murderous blue laughter

Starching and cleaning
O yes scolding and wheedling
pressing little white heads
against her big-aproned breasts
seeing down to the smallest fed
feeding her own children on Satanic bread

But this fat black woman ain't no Jemima
                Sure thing Honey/Yeah

Alone

The fat black woman
sits alone
gathering
gathering
into herself
onto herself
soft stone
woman moan
the fat black woman
sits alone
gathering
gathering
into herself
onto herself
drift dome
river foam
the fat black woman
sits alone
gathering
gathering
into herself
onto herself

     gathering gathering
     gathering gathering
     gathering gathering

       silence

The Fat Black Woman Goes Shopping

Shopping in London winter
is a real drag for the fat black woman
going from store to store
in search of accommodating clothes
and de weather so cold

Look at the frozen thin mannequins
fixing her with grin
and de pretty face salesgals
exchanging slimming glances
thinking she don't notice

Lord is aggravating

Nothing soft and bright and billowing
to flow like breezy sunlight
when she walking

The fat black woman curses in Swahili/Yoruba
and nation language under her breathing
all this journeying and journeying

The fat black woman could only conclude
that when it come to fashion
the choice is lean

      Nothing much beyond size 14

Invitation

1

If my fat
was too much for me
I would have told you
I would have lost a stone
or two

I would have gone jogging
even when it was fogging
I would have weighed in
sitting the bathroom scale
with my tail tucked in

I would have dieted
more care than a diabetic

But as it is
I'm feeling fine
feel no need
to change my lines
when I move I'm target light

Come up and see me sometime

2

Come up and see me sometime
Come up and see me sometime

My breasts are huge exciting
amnions of watermelon
                    your hands can't cup
my thighs are twin seals
                    fat slick pups
there's a purple cherry
below the blues
                    of my black seabelly
there's a mole that gets a ride
each time I shift the heritage
of my behind

Come up and see me sometime

Trap Evasions

Refusing to be a model
of her own affliction
the fat black woman steers clear
of circles that lead nowhere

evades:

bushswamps
quicksands
cesspits
treadmills
bride ties
grave lies

Men who only see
a spring of children
in her thighs
when there are mountains
in her mites

Thoughts drifting through the fat black woman's head while having a full bubble bath

Steatopygous sky
Steatopygous sea
Steatopygous waves
Steatopygous me

O how I long to place my foot
on the head of anthropology

to swig my breasts
in the face of history

to scrub my back
with the dogma of theology

to put my soap
in the slimming industry's
profitsome spoke

Steatopygous sky
Steatopygous sea
Steatopygous waves
Steatopygous me

The Fat Black Woman Composes a
Black Poem . . .

Black as the intrusion
of a rude wet tongue

Black as the boldness
of a quick home run

Black as the blackness
of a rolling ship

Black as the sweetness
of black orchid milk

Black as the token
of my ancestors bread

Black as the beauty
of the nappy head

Black as the blueness
of a swift backlash

Black as the spraying
of a reggae sunsplash

Handwritten annotations:

associates pink with
a tongue that in
neither dry or exhausted
but one that
has finally spoken
out after being
silent.

parallel
new sense
of black
identity.

colour white
mothers
milk

Nichols redef
'Black'

Her excessive
use of colours and
irony is her way
of transforming
female subjectivity
her language and
style suggest mul
desires' — May
evoke a feeling
of excess
conveyed thr
a repetitive se

The metre in the last line
ensures the word 'sunsplash'
said in a west indian accen
emphasis on last syllable 'plash

= yellow sunshine & music ⟺ black

suggest her inner spiritua
strength through subverted
smile, the heaviness of her
fat body.

. . . And a Fat Poem

Fat is
as fat is
as fat is

Fat does
as fat thinks

Fat feels
as fat please

Fat believes

        Fat is to butter
        as milk is to cream
        fat is to sugar
        as pud is to steam

Fat is a dream
in times of lean

        fat is a darling
        a dumpling
        a squeeze
        fat is cuddles
        up a baby's sleeve

        and fat speaks for itself

igorous tone sheer vitality and
advance — Her 'fat self' is also an ubiquitous
abashed black woman with extraordinary
self confidence & control.

The Fat Black Woman's Motto on Her Bedroom Door

IT'S BETTER TO DIE IN THE FLESH OF HOPE
THAN TO LIVE IN THE SLIMNESS OF DESPAIR

Tropical Death

The fat black woman want
a brilliant tropical death
not a cold sojourn
in some North Europe far/forlorn

The fat black woman want
some heat/hibiscus at her feet
blue sea dress
to wrap her neat

The fat black woman want
some bawl
no quiet jerk tear wiping
a polite hearse withdrawal

The fat black woman want
all her dead rights
first night
third night
nine night
all the sleepless droning
red-eyed wake nights

In the heart
of her mother's sweetbreast
In the shade
of the sun leaf's cool bless
In the bloom
of her people's bloodrest

the fat black woman want
a brilliant tropical death yes

Looking at Miss World

Tonight the fat black woman
is all agaze
will some Miss (plump at least
if not fat and black) uphold her name

The fat black woman awaits in vain
slim after slim aspirant appears
baring her treasures in hopeful despair
this the fat black woman can hardly bear

And as the beauties yearn
and the beauties yearn
the fat black woman wonders
when will the beauties
ever really burn

O the night wears on
the night wears on
judges mingling with chiffons

The fat black woman gets up
and pours some gin
toasting herself as a likely win

The Fat Black Woman's Instructions to a Suitor

Do the boggie-woggie
Do the hop
Do the Charlestown
Do the rock
Do the chicken funky
Do the foxtrot

Do the tango
Drop yourself like a mango
Do the minuet
Spin me a good ole pirouette
Do the highland fling
Get down baby
Do that limbo thing

After doing all that, and maybe mo
hope you have a little energy left
to carry me across the threshold

The Fat Black Woman Versus Politics

The fat black woman
could see through politicians
like snake sees through rat
she knows the oil
that ease the tongue
she knows the soup-mouth tact
she knows the game
the lame race for fame
she knows the slippery hammer
wearing down upon the brain

In dreams she's seen them
stalking the corridors of power
faces behind a ballot-box cover
the fat black woman won't be their lover

But if you were to ask her
What's your greatest political ambition?
she'll be sure to answer

>   To feed powercrazy politicians a manifesto of lard
>   To place my X against a bowl of custard

Small Questions Asked by the Fat Black Woman

Will the rains
cleanse the earth of shrapnel
and wasted shells

will the seas
toss up bright fish
in wave on wave of toxic shoal

will the waters
seep the shore

feeding slowly the greying
angry roots

will trees bear fruit

will I like Eve
be tempted once again
if I survive

Afterword

The fat black woman
will come out of the forest
brushing vegetations
from the shorn of her hair

flaunting waterpearls
in the bush of her thighs
blushing wet in the morning
                               sunlight

the fat black woman will sigh
there will be an immense joy
in the full of her eye
as she beholds

behold now the fat black woman
who will come out of the forest

when the last of her race
is finally and utterly extinguished

when the wind pushes back the last curtain
of male white blindness

the fat black woman will emerge
and tremblingly fearlessly

stake her claim again

In Spite of Ourselves

Like a Beacon

In London
every now and then
I get this craving
for my mother's food
I leave art galleries
in search of plantains
saltfish/sweet potatoes

I need this link

I need this touch
of home
swinging my bag
like a beacon
against the cold

Fear

Our culture rub skin
against your own
bruising awkward as plums

black music enrich
food spice up

You say you're civilised
a kind of pride
ask, 'Are you going back sometime?'

but of course
home is where the heart lies

I come from a backyard
where the sun reaches down
mangoes fall to the ground
politicians turn cruel clowns

And here? Here

sometimes I grow afraid
too many young blacks
reaping seconds
indignant cities full of jail

I think my child's too loving
for this fear

Island Man

(for a Caribbean island man in London who still wakes up to the sound of the sea)

Morning
and island man wakes up
to the sound of blue surf
in his head
the steady breaking and wombing

wild seabirds
and fishermen pushing out to sea
the sun surfacing defiantly

from the east
of his small emerald island
he always comes back   groggily groggily

Comes back to sands
of a grey metallic soar
                         to surge of wheels
to dull North Circular roar

muffling muffling
his crumpled pillow waves
island man heaves himself

Another London day

We New World Blacks

The timbre
in our voice
betrays us
however far
we've been

whatever tongue
we speak
the old ghost
asserts itself
in dusky echoes

like driftwood
traces

and in spite of
ourselves
we know the way
back to

the river stone

the little decayed
spirit
of the navel string
hiding in our back garden

*such language hybridization
succinctly dramatises a rupture
with some myths & metaphors that
have relegated black women to
a space of endless forgiveness,
weakness and similarity.*

*Actually breaks down the
'solid' english language.*

Shopping

I'm guilty of buying too little food

1 carton milk
1 carton juice
1 half chicken
a little veg and fruit

Why can't you buy
for more than one day
at a time
my old man whines

Still blank as a zombie
I wander supermarket aisles

The chunky red odours
behind the cellophane
cannot revive
the spritely apples
the lady reluctantly urging samples

Between the bulge of the shelf
and the cast of my eye
between the nerve of my trolley
and the will of my mind
I'm always paralysed

Winter Thoughts

I've reduced the sun
to the neat oblong of fire
in my living room

I've reduced the little
fleshy tongues of the vagina
to the pimpled grate
and the reddening licking
flames

I've reduced the sea
to the throbbing fruit
in me

And outside
the old rose tree
is once again winterdying

While I lay here sprawled
thinking
how sex and death
are always at the heart
of living

Skanking Englishman Between Trains

Met him at Birmingham Station
small yellow hair Englishman
hi fi stereo swinging in one hand
walking in rhythm to reggae sound/Man

he was alive
he was full-o-jive
said he had a lovely
Jamaican wife

Said he couldn't remember
the taste of English food
I like mih drops
me johnny cakes
me peas and rice
me soup/Man

he was alive
he was full-o-jive
said he had a lovely
Jamaican wife

Said, showing me her photo
whenever we have a little quarrel
you know/to sweeten her up
I surprise her with a nice mango/Man

he was alive
he was full-o-jive
said he had a lovely Jamaican wife

Spring

After two unpredictable spells
of influenza that winter
I was taking no chances
(not even to put the rubbish outside)

pulling on my old black jacket
resolutely winding
a scarf round and round my neck
winter rituals I had grown to
accept
with all the courage of an unemerged
butterfly
I unbolted the door and stepped outside

only to have that daffodil baby
kick me in the eye

Two Old Black Men
on a Leicester Square Park Bench

What do you dream of you
old black men sitting
on park benches staunchly
wrapped up in scarves
and coats of silence
eyes far away from the cold
grey and strutting
pigeon
ashy fingers trembling
(though it's said that the old
hardly ever feel the cold)

do you dream revolutions
you could have forged
or mourn
some sunfull woman you
might have known a
hibiscus flower
ghost memories of desire

O it's easy
to rainbow the past
after all the letters from
home spoke of hardships

and the sun was traded long ago

Waiting for Thelma's Laughter

(for Thelma, my West Indian born Afro-American neighbour)

You wanna take the world
in hand
and fix-it-up
the way you fix your living room

You wanna reach out and crush
life's big and small injustices
in the fire and honey
of your hands

You wanna scream
cause your head's too small
for your dreams

and the children
       running round
          acting like lil clowns
             breaking the furniture down

while I sit through
it all watching you
knowing any time now
your laughter's gonna come

to drown and heal us all

Back Home Contemplation

Those Women

Cut and contriving women
hauling fresh shrimps
up in their seines

standing waist deep
in the brown voluptuous
water of their own element

how I remember those women
sweeping in the childish rivers
of my eyes

and the fish slipping
like eels
through their laughing thighs

Childhood

My childhood
was a watershed of sunlight
and strange recurring mysteries

the fishes before a drought
came in droves
floundering at our backdoors

saltwater drove them in
moving groggy shadows
beneath the mirror surfacing

sunfish/patwa/butterfish
half stunned I watched
bare hand I gripped

at Sunday school
we didn't learn to pray
for the dying freshwater souls of fish

Back Home Contemplation

There is more to heaven
than meet the eye
there is more to sea
than watch the sky
there is more to earth
than dream the mind

O my eye

The heavens are blue
but the sun is murderous
the sea is calm
but the waves reap havoc
the earth is firm
but trees dance shadows
and bush eyes turn

Price We Pay for the Sun

These islands
not picture postcards
for unravelling tourist
you know
these islands real
more real
than flesh and blood
past stone
past foam
these islands split
bone

my mother's breasts
like sleeping volcanoes
who know
what kinda sulph-furious
cancer tricking her
below
while the wind
constantly whipping
my father's tears
to salty hurricanes
and my grandmothers croon
sifting sand
water mirroring palm

Poverty is the price
we pay for the sun girl
run come

So the Eagle

(on the death of the Grenadian revolution)

So the eagle
has turned full circle
again
swooping on a revolution's
remains
winging bullets/burgers/
hot rescues
in the claws of its rein

Praise Song for My Mother

You were
water to me
deep and bold and fathoming

You were
moon's eye to me
pull and grained and mantling

You were
sunrise to me
rise and warm and streaming

You were
the fishes red gill to me
the flame tree's spread to me
the crab's leg/the fried plantain smell
                              replenishing replenishing

Go to your wide futures, you said

Why Shouldn't She?

My mother loved cooking
but hated washing up
Why shouldn't she?
cooking was an art
she could move her lips to
then the pleasure
feeding the proverbial
multitude (us)
on less than a loaf
and two fishes

Hey There Now!

(for Lesley)

Hey there now
my brownwater flower
     my sunchild branching
from my mountain river
     hey there now!
my young stream
       headlong
         rushing
I love to watch you
     when you're
       sleeping
         blushing

Candlefly

The candlefly
always came at night
blinking the ceiling
with its small searchlight

as a child I stared up
uneasily through the darkness
remembering the old folk saying

Candlefly means
a stranger will come
a stranger will visit

still I couldn't be comforted
the candlefly was both a magic
and a menace

a creature with a mission

a flickering stranger

                    not unlike death

Mango

Have a mango
sweet rainwashed sunripe
mango
that the birds themselves
woulda pick
if only they had seen it
a rosy miracle

Here
take it from mih hand

Star-apple

Deepest purple
or pale green white
the star-apple is a sweet fruit
with a sweet star brimming centre
and a turn back skin
that always left me sweetly
sticky mouth

Guenips

Guenips
hanging in abundant
bunches on the fat knuckled
guenip tree
Guenips
melting like small moons
on my tongue
the succulent green gold
of the fruit kingdom

Sea Timeless Song

Hurricane come
and hurricane go
but sea . . . sea timeless
sea timeless
sea timeless
sea timeless
sea timeless

Hibiscus bloom
then dry-wither so
but sea . . . sea timeless
sea timeless
sea timeless
sea timeless
sea timeless

Tourist come
and tourist go
but sea . . . sea timeless
sea timeless
sea timeless
sea timeless
sea timeless

Be a Butterfly

Don't be a kyatta-pilla
Be a butterfly
old preacher screamed
to illustrate his sermon
of Jesus and the higher life

rivulets of well-earned
sweat sliding down
his muscly mahogany face
in the half-empty school church
we sat shaking with muffling
laughter
watching our mother trying to save
herself from joining the wave

only our father remaining poker face
and afterwards we always went home to
split peas Sunday soup
with dumplings, fufu and pigtail

Don't be a kyatta-pilla
Be a butterfly
Be a butterfly

That was de life preacher
and you was right

Iguana Memory

Saw an iguana once
when I was very small
in our backdam backyard
came rustling across my path

green like moving newleaf sunlight

big like big big lizard
with more legs than centipede
so it seemed to me
and it must have stopped a while
eyes meeting mine
iguana and child locked in a brief
split moment happening
before it went hurrying

       for the green of its life

from
i is a long memoried woman

Waterpot

The daily going out
and coming in
always being hurried
along
like like . . . cattle

In the evenings
returning from the fields
she tried hard to walk
like a woman

she tried very hard
pulling herself erect
with every three or four
steps
pulling herself together
holding herself like
royal cane

And the overseer
hurrying them along
in the quickening darkness

And the overseer sneering
them along in the quickening
darkness
sneered at the pathetic
the pathetic display
of dignity

O but look
there's a waterpot growing
from her head

53

Loveact

She enter into his Great House
her see-far looking eyes
unassuming

He fix her with his glassy stare
and feel the thin fire in his blood
awakening

Soon she is the fuel
that keep them all going

He/his mistresswife/and his
children who take to her breasts
like leeches

He want to tower above her
want her to raise her ebony
haunches and when she does
he think she can be trusted
and drinks her in

and his mistresswife
spending her days in rings
of vacant smiling
is glad to be rid of the
loveact

But time pass/es

Her sorcery cut them
like a whip

She hide her triumph
and slowly stir the hate
of poison in

she doesn't love him

Skin-teeth

Not every skin-teeth
is a smile 'Massa'

if you see me smiling
when you pass

if you see me bending
when you ask

Know that I smile
know that I bend

only the better
to rise and strike
again

Sugar Cane

1

There is something
about sugar cane

he isn't what
he seem –

indifferent hard
and sheathed in blades

his waving arms
is a sign for help

his skin thick
only to protect
the juice inside
himself

2

His colour
is the aura
of jaundice
when he ripe

he shiver
like ague
when it rain

he suffer
from bellywork
burning fever
and delirium

just before
the hurricane
strike
smashing him to pieces

56

[handwritten annotations:]
Personifies the sugar cane as male.
on outside
inside is soft
male slaves task
yellow eyes
ripe fruit grows/cha[nges]
chill/feverish sensation.
nature causes sugar cane to be destroye[d]
eg the slave is tortured.

3

Growing up
is an art

he don't have
any control of

it is us
who groom and
weed him

who stick him
in the earth
in the first place

and when he
growing tall

with the help
of the sun
and rain

we feel the
need to strangle
the life

out of him

But either way he can't survive

eg wait for something grow before you kill it - terrible murderous image.

1 word per line gives impression of something growing slowly.

4
Slowly
pain-
fully
sugar
cane
pushes
his
knotted
joints
upwards
from
the
earth
slowly
pain-
fully
he
comes
to learn
the
truth
about
himself
the
crimes
committed
in
his
name

5

He cast his shadow
to the earth

the wind is
his only mistress

I hear them
moving
in rustling tones

she shakes
his hard reserve

smoothing
stroking
caressing
all his length
shamelessly

I crouch
below them
quietly

[handwritten annotations:]
soothing, allows him to feel sensitive.

sexual connotations. personified as well.

sybillance.

→ secretive / hiding

about to chop down the sugar cane / kill the slave.

Like a Flame

Raising up
from my weeding
of ripening cane

my eyes
make four
with this man

there ain't
no reason
to laugh

but
I laughing
in confusion

his hands
soft his words
quick his lips
curling as in
prayer

I nod

I like this man

Tonight
I go to meet him
like a flame

This Kingdom

This Kingdom Will Not Reign
Forever

Cool winds blow
softly

in brilliant sunshine
fruits pulse
flowers flame

mountains shade to
purple

the Great House
with its palm and orange
groves

sturdy

and the sea encircling
all
is a spectrum of blue
jewels
shimmering and skirting

But Beware

Soft winds can turn
volatile
can merge with rains
can turn hurricane

Mountains can erupt
sulphur springs
bubbling quick
and hot

like bile spilling
from a witch's cauldron

Swamps can send plagues –
dysentery, fevers

plantations can perish

lands turn barren

And the white man
no longer at ease
with the faint drum/
beat

no longer indifferent
to the sweating sun/
heat

can leave exhausted
or
turn his thoughts
to death

And we
the rage growing
like the chiggers
in our feet

can wait
or
take our freedom

whatever happens

**This Kingdom Will Not Reign
Forever**

Holding My Beads

Unforgiving as the course of justice
Inerasable as my scars and fate
I am here
a woman . . . with all my lives
strung out like beads
                    before me

It isn't privilege or pity
that I seek
It isn't reverence or safety
quick happiness or purity
                    but
the power to be what I am/   a woman
charting my own futures/   a woman
holding my beads in my hand

Epilogue

I have crossed an ocean
I have lost my tongue
from the root of the old one
a new one has sprung